The Black Riders and Other Lines, and War is Kind

Stephen Crane

THE BLACK RIDERS AND
OTHER LINES

BY
STEPHEN CRANE

LONDON WILLIAM HEINEMANN
MDCCCXCVI
PRINTED BY JOHN WILSON AND SON
CAMBRIDGE U.S.A.

TO HAMLIN GARLAND

I

Black riders came from the sea.
There was clang and clang of spear and shield,
And clash and clash of hoof and heel,
Wild shouts and the wave of hair
In the rush upon the wind:
Thus the ride of sin.

II

Three little birds in a row
Sat musing.
A man passed near that place.
Then did the little birds nudge each other.

They said, "He thinks he can sing."
They threw back their heads to laugh.
With quaint countenances
They regarded him.
They were very curious,
Those three little birds in a row.

III

In the desert
I saw a creature, naked, bestial,
who, squatting upon the ground,
Held his heart in his hands,
And ate of it.
I said, "Is it good, friend?"

"It is bitter — bitter," he answered;
"But I like it
Because it is bitter,
And because it is my heart."

IV

Yes, I have a thousand tongues,
And nine and ninety-nine lie.
Though I strive to use the one,
It will make no melody at my will,
But is dead in my mouth.

V

Once there came a man
Who said,
"Range me all men of the world in rows."
And instantly
There was terrific clamour among the people
Against being ranged in rows.
There was a loud quarrel, world-wide.
It endured for ages;
And blood was shed
By those who would not stand in rows,
And by those who pined to stand in rows.
Eventually, the man went to death, weeping.
And those who staid in bloody scuffle
Knew not the great simplicity.

VI

God fashioned the ship of the world carefully.
With the infinite skill of an All-Master
Made He the hull and the sails,
Held He the rudder
Ready for adjustment.
Erect stood He, scanning His work proudly.
Then — at fateful time — a wrong called,
And God turned, heeding.
Lo, the ship, at this opportunity, slipped slyly,
Making cunning noiseless travel down the ways.
So that, forever rudderless, it went upon the seas
Going ridiculous voyages,
Making quaint progress,

Turning as with serious purpose
Before stupid winds.
And there were many in the sky
Who laughed at this thing.

VII

Mystic shadow, bending near me,
Who art thou?
Whence come ye?
And — tell me — is it fair
Or is the truth bitter as eaten fire?
Tell me!
Fear not that I should quaver.
For I dare — I dare.
Then, tell me!

VIII

I looked here;
I looked there;
Nowhere could I see my love.
And — this time —
She was in my heart.
Truly, then, I have no complaint,
For though she be fair and fairer,
She is none so fair as she
In my heart.

IX

I stood upon a high place,
And saw, below, many devils
Running, leaping,
and carousing in sin.
One looked up, grinning,
And said, "Comrade! Brother!"

X

Should the wide world roll away,
Leaving black terror,
Limitless night,
Nor God, nor man, nor place to stand
Would be to me essential,
If thou and thy white arms were there,
And the fall to doom a long way.

XI

In a lonely place,
I encountered a sage
Who sat, all still,
Regarding a newspaper.
He accosted me:
"Sir, what is this?"
Then I saw that I was greater,
Aye, greater than this sage.
I answered him at once,
"Old, old man, it is the wisdom of the age."
The sage looked upon me with admiration.

XII

"And the sins of the fathers shall be
visited upon the heads of the children,
even unto the third and fourth
generation of them that hate me."

Well, then I hate thee, unrighteous picture;
Wicked image, I hate thee;
So, strike with thy vengeance
The heads of those little men
Who come blindly.
It will be a brave thing.

XIII

If there is a witness to my little life,
To my tiny throes and struggles,

He sees a fool;
And it is not fine for gods to menace fools.

XIV

There was crimson clash of war.
Lands turned black and bare;
Women wept;
Babes ran, wondering.
There came one who understood not these things.
He said, "Why is this?"
Whereupon a million strove to answer him.
There was such intricate clamour of tongues,
That still the reason was not.

XV

"Tell brave deeds of war."
Then they recounted tales, —
"There were stern stands
And bitter runs for glory."
Ah, I think there were braver deeds.

XVI

Charity thou art a lie,
A toy of women,
A pleasure of certain men.
In the presence of justice,
Lo, the walls of the temple
Are visible
Through thy form of sudden shadows.

XVII

There were many who went in huddled procession,
They knew not whither;
But, at any rate, success or calamity
Would attend all in equality.

There was one who sought a new road.
He went into direful thickets,
And ultimately he died thus, alone;
But they said he had courage.

XVIII

In heaven,
Some little blades of grass
Stood before God.
"What did you do?"
Then all save one of the little blades
Began eagerly to relate
The merits of their lives.
This one stayed a small way behind,
Ashamed.
Presently, God said,
"And what did you do?"
The little blade answered, "Oh my Lord,
Memory is bitter to me,
For, if I did good deeds,
I know not of them."
Then God, in all His splendor,
Arose from His throne.
"Oh, best little blade of grass!" He said.

XIX

A god in wrath
Was beating a man;
He cuffed him loudly
With thunderous blows
That rang and rolled over the earth.
All people came running.
The man screamed and struggled,
And bit madly at the feet of the god.
The people cried,
"Ah, what a wicked man!"
And —
"Ah, what a redoubtable god!"

XX

A learned man came to me once.
He said, "I know the way, — come."
And I was overjoyed at this.
Together we hastened.
Soon, too soon, were we
Where my eyes were useless,
And I knew not the ways of my feet.
I clung to the hand of my friend;
But at last he cried, "I am lost."

XXI

There was, before me,
Mile upon mile
Of snow, ice, burning sand.

And yet I could look beyond all this,
To a place of infinite beauty;
And I could see the loveliness of her
Who walked in the shade of the trees.
When I gazed,
All was lost
But this place of beauty and her.
When I gazed,
And in my gazing, desired,
Then came again
Mile upon mile,
Of snow, ice, burning sand.

XXII

Once I saw mountains angry,
And ranged in battle-front.
Against them stood a little man;
Aye, he was no bigger than my finger.
I laughed, and spoke to one near me,
"Will he prevail?"
"Surely," replied this other;
"His grandfathers beat them many times."
Then did I see much virtue in grandfathers —
At least, for the little man
Who stood against the mountains.

XXIII

Places among the stars,
Soft gardens near the sun,
Keep your distant beauty;

Shed no beams upon my weak heart.
Since she is here
In a place of blackness,
Not your golden days
Nor your silver nights
Can call me to you.
Since she is here
In a place of blackness,
Here I stay and wait

XXIV

I saw a man pursuing the horizon;
Round and round they sped.
I was disturbed at this;
I accosted the man.
"It is futile," I said,
"You can never — "

"You lie," he cried,
And ran on.

XXV

Behold, the grave of a wicked man,
And near it, a stern spirit.

There came a drooping maid with violets,
But the spirit grasped her arm.
"No flowers for him," he said.
The maid wept:
"Ah, I loved him."

But the spirit, grim and frowning:
"No flowers for him."

Now, this is it —
If the spirit was just,
Why did the maid weep?

XXVI

There was set before me a mighty hill,
And long days I climbed
Through regions of snow.
When I had before me the summit-view,
It seemed that my labour
Had been to see gardens
Lying at impossible distances.

XXVII

A youth in apparel that glittered
Went to walk in a grim forest.
There he met an assassin
Attired all in garb of old days;
He, scowling through the thickets,
And dagger poised quivering,
Rushed upon the youth.
"Sir," said this latter,
"I am enchanted, believe me,
To die, thus,
In this medieval fashion,
According to the best legends;
Ah, what joy!"

Then took he the wound, smiling,
And died, content.

XXVIII

"Truth," said a traveller,
"Is a rock, a mighty fortress;
Often have I been to it,
Even to its highest tower,
From whence the world looks black."

"Truth," said a traveller,
"Is a breath, a wind,
A shadow, a phantom;
Long have I pursued it,
But never have I touched
The hem of its garment."

And I believed the second traveller;
For truth was to me
A breath, a wind,
A shadow, a phantom,
And never had I touched
The hem of its garment.

XXIX

Behold, from the land of the farther suns
I returned.
And I was in a reptile-swarming place,
Peopled, otherwise, with grimaces,
Shrouded above in black impenetrableness.

I shrank, loathing,
Sick with it.
And I said to him,
"What is this?"
He made answer slowly,
"Spirit, this is a world;
This was your home."

XXX

Supposing that I should have the courage
To let a red sword of virtue
Plunge into my heart,
Letting to the weeds of the ground
My sinful blood,
What can you offer me?
A gardened castle?
A flowery kingdom?

What? A hope?
Then hence with your red sword of virtue.

XXXI

Many workmen
Built a huge ball of masonry
Upon a mountain-top.
Then they went to the valley below,
And turned to behold their work.
"It is grand," they said;
They loved the thing.

Of a sudden, it moved:
It came upon them swiftly;
It crushed them all to blood.
But some had opportunity to squeal.

XXXII

Two or three angels
Came near to the earth.
They saw a fat church.
Little black streams of people
Came and went in continually.
And the angels were puzzled
To know why the people went thus,
And why they stayed so long within.

XXXIII

There was one I met upon the road
Who looked at me with kind eyes.
Her said, "Show me of your wares."
And this I did,
Holding forth one.
He said, "It is a sin."
Then held I forth another;
He said, "It is a sin."
Then held I forth another;
He said, "It is a sin."
And so to the end;
Always he said, "It is a sin."
And, finally, I cried out,
"But I have none other."

Then did he look at me
With kinder eyes.
"Poor soul!" he said.

XXXIV

I stood upon a highway,
And, behold, there came
Many strange peddlers.
To me each one made gestures,
Holding forth little images, saying,
"This is my pattern of God.
Now this is the God I prefer."

But I said, "Hence!
Leave me with mine own,
And take you yours away;
I can't buy of your patterns of God,
The little gods you may rightly prefer."

XXXV

A man saw a ball of gold in the sky;
He climbed for it,
And eventually he achieved it —
It was clay.

Now this is the strange part:
When the man went to the earth
And looked again,
Lo, there was the ball of gold.
Now this is the strange part:

It was a ball of gold.
Aye, by the heavens, it was a ball of gold.

XXXVI

I met a seer.
He held in his hands
The book of wisdom.
"Sir," I addressed him,
"Let me read."
"Child — " he began.
"Sir," I said,
"Think not that I am a child,
For already I know much
Of that which you hold.
Aye, much."

He smiled.
Then he opened the book
And held it before me. —
Strange that I should have grown so suddenly blind.

XXXVII

On the horizon the peaks assembled;
And as I looked,
The march of the mountains began.
As they marched, they sang,
"Aye! We come! We come!"

XXXVIII

The ocean said to me once,
"Look!
Yonder on the shore
Is a woman, weeping.
I have watched her.
Go you and tell her this —
Her lover I have laid
In cool green hall.
There is wealth of golden sand
And pillars, coral-red;
Two white fish stand guard at his bier.

"Tell her this
And more —
That the king of the seas
Weeps too, old, helpless man.
The bustling fates

Heap his hands with corpses
Until he stands like a child
With a surplus of toys."

XXXIX

The livid lightnings flashed in the clouds;
The leaden thunders crashed.
A worshipper raised his arm.
"Hearken! Hearken! The voice of God!"

"Not so," said a man.

"The voice of God whispers in the heart
So softly
That the soul pauses,
Making no noise,
And strives for these melodies,
Distant, sighing, like faintest breath,
And all the being is still to hear."

XL

And you love me

I love you.

You are, then, cold coward.

Aye; but, beloved,
When I strive to come to you,
Man's opinions, a thousand thickets,
My interwoven existence,
My life,
Caught in the stubble of the world
Like a tender veil —
This stays me.
No strange move can I make
Without noise of tearing
I dare not.

If love loves,
There is no world

Nor word.
All is lost
Save thought of love
And place to dream.
You love me?

I love you.

You are, then, cold coward.

Aye; but, beloved —

XLI

Love walked alone.
The rocks cut her tender feet,
And the brambles tore her fair limbs.
There came a companion to her,
But, alas, he was no help,
For his name was heart's pain.

XLII

I walked in a desert.
And I cried,
"Ah, God, take me from this place!"
A voice said, "It is no desert."
I cried, "Well, But —
The sand, the heat, the vacant horizon."
A voice said, "It is no desert."

XLIII

There came whisperings in the winds:
"Good-bye! Good-bye!"
Little voices called in the darkness:
"Good-bye! Good-bye!"
Then I stretched forth my arms.
"No — no — "
There came whisperings in the wind
"Good-bye! Good-bye!"
Little voices called in the darkness:
"Good-bye! Good-bye!"

XLIV

I was in the darkness;
I could not see my words
Nor the wishes of my heart.
Then suddenly there was a great light —

"Let me into the darkness again."

XLV

Tradition, thou art for suckling children,
Thou art the enlivening milk for babes;
But no meat for men is in thee.
Then —
But, alas, we all are babes.

XLVI

Many red devils ran from my heart
And out upon the page,
They were so tiny
The pen could mash them.
And many struggled in the ink.
It was strange
To write in this red muck
Of things from my heart.

XLVII

"Think as I think," said a man,
"Or you are abominably wicked;
You are a toad."

And after I had thought of it,
I said, "I will, then, be a toad."

XLVIII

Once there was a man —
Oh, so wise!
In all drink
He detected the bitter,
And in all touch
He found the sting.
At last he cried thus:
"There is nothing —
No life,
No joy,

No pain —
There is nothing save opinion,
And opinion be damned."

XLIX

I stood musing in a black world,
Not knowing where to direct my feet.
And I saw the quick stream of men
Pouring ceaselessly,
Filled with eager faces,
A torrent of desire.
I called to them,
"Where do you go? What do you see?"
A thousand voices called to me.
A thousand fingers pointed.
"Look! look! There!"

I know not of it.
But, lo! In the far sky shone a radiance
Ineffable, divine —
A vision painted upon a pall;
And sometimes it was,
And sometimes it was not.
I hesitated.

Then from the stream
Came roaring voices,
Impatient:
"Look! look! There!"

So again I saw,

And leaped, unhesitant,
And struggled and fumed
With outspread clutching fingers.
The hard hills tore my flesh;
The ways bit my feet.
At last I looked again.
No radiance in the far sky,
Ineffable, divine;
No vision painted upon a pall;
And always my eyes ached for the light.
Then I cried in despair,
"I see nothing! Oh, where do I go?"
The torrent turned again its faces:
"Look! look! There!"
And at the blindness of my spirit
They screamed,
"Fool! fool! fool!"

L

You say you are holy,
And that
Because I have not seen you sin.
Aye, but there are those
Who see you sin, my friend.

LI

A man went before a strange God —
The God of many men, sadly wise.
And the deity thundered loudly,
Fat with rage, and puffing.

"Kneel, mortal, and cringe
And grovel and do homage
To My Particularly Sublime Majesty."

The man fled.

Then the man went to another God —
The God of his inner thoughts.
And this one looked at him
With soft eyes
Lit with infinite comprehension,
And said, "My poor child!"

LII

Why do you strive for greatness, fool?
Go pluck a bough and wear it.
It is as sufficing.

My Lord, there are certain barbarians
Who tilt their noses
As if the stars were flowers,
And Thy servant is lost among their shoe-buckles.
Fain would I have mine eyes even with their eyes.

Fool, go pluck a bough and wear it.

LIII

i

Blustering God,
Stamping across the sky

With loud swagger,
I fear You not.
No, though from Your highest heaven
You plunge Your spear at my heart,
I fear You not.
No, not if the blow
Is as the lightning blasting a tree,
I fear You not, puffing braggart.

ii

If Thou canst see into my heart
That I fear Thee not,
Thou wilt see why I fear Thee not,
And why it is right.

So threaten not, Thou, with Thy bloody spears,
Else Thy sublime ears shall hear curses.

iii

Withal, there is One whom I fear:
I fear to see grief upon that face.
Perchance, friend, He is not your God;
If so, spit upon Him.
By it you will do no profanity.
But I —
Ah, sooner would I die
Than see tears in those eyes of my soul.

LIV

"It was wrong to do this," said the angel.
"You should live like a flower,
Holding malice like a puppy,
Waging war like a lambkin."

"Not so," quoth the man
Who had no fear of spirits;
"It is only wrong for angels
Who can live like the flowers,
Holding malice like the puppies,
Waging war like the lambkins."

LV

A man toiled on a burning road,
Never resting.
Once he saw a fat, stupid ass
Grinning at him from a green place.
The man cried out in rage,
"Ah! Do not deride me, fool!
I know you —
All day stuffing your belly,
Burying your heart
In grass and tender sprouts:
It will not suffice you."
But the ass only grinned at him from the green place.

LVI

A man feared that he might find an assassin;
Another that he might find a victim.
One was more wise than the other.

LVII

With eye and with gesture
You say you are holy.
I say you lie;
For I did see you
Draw away your coats
From the sin upon the hands
Of a little child.
Liar!

LVIII

The sage lectured brilliantly.
Before him, two images:
"Now this one is a devil,
And this one is me."
He turned away.
Then a cunning pupil
Changed the positions.
Turned the sage again:
"Now this one is a devil,
And this one is me."
The pupils sat, all grinning,
And rejoiced in the game.
But the sage was a sage.

LIX

Walking in the sky,
A man in strange black garb
Encountered a radiant form.
Then his steps were eager;
Bowed he devoutly.
"My Lord," said he.
But the spirit knew him not.

LX

Upon the road of my life,
Passed me many fair creatures,
Clothed all in white, and radiant.
To one, finally, I made speech:
"Who art thou?"
But she, like the others,
Kept cowled her face,
And answered in haste, anxiously,
"I am good deed, forsooth;
You have often seen me."
"Not uncowled," I made reply.
And with rash and strong hand,
Though she resisted,
I drew away the veil
And gazed at the features of vanity.
She, shamefaced, went on;
And after I had mused a time,
I said of myself,
          "Fool!"

LXI

i

There was a man and a woman
Who sinned.
Then did the man heap the punishment
All upon the head of her,
And went away gaily.

ii

There was a man and a woman
Who sinned.
And the man stood with her.
As upon her head, so upon his,
Fell blow and blow,
And all people screaming, "Fool!"
He was a brave heart.

iii

He was a brave heart.
Would you speak with him, friend?
Well, he is dead,
And there went your opportunity.
Let it be your grief
That he is dead
And your opportunity gone;
For, in that, you were a coward.

LXII

There was a man who lived a life of fire.
Even upon the fabric of time,
Where purple becomes orange
And orange purple,
This life glowed,
A dire red stain, indelible;
Yet when he was dead,
He saw that he had not lived.

LXIII

There was a great cathedral.
To solemn songs,
A white procession
Moved toward the altar.
The chief man there
Was erect, and bore himself proudly.
Yet some could see him cringe,
As in a place of danger,
Throwing frightened glances into the air,
A-start at threatening faces of the past.

LXIV

Friend, your white beard sweeps the ground.
Why do you stand, expectant?
Do you hope to see it
In one of your withered days?
With your old eyes
Do you hope to see

The triumphal march of justice?
Do not wait, friend!
Take your white beard
And your old eyes
To more tender lands.

LXV

Once, I knew a fine song,
— It is true, believe me —
It was all of birds,
And I held them in a basket;
When I opened the wicket,
Heavens! They all flew away.
I cried, "Come back, little thoughts!"
But they only laughed.
They flew on
Until they were as sand
Thrown between me and the sky.

LXVI

If I should cast off this tattered coat,
And go free into the mighty sky;
If I should find nothing there
But a vast blue,
Echoless, ignorant —
What then?

LXVII

God lay dead in heaven;
Angels sang the hymn of the end;

Purple winds went moaning,
Their wings drip-dripping
With blood
That fell upon the earth.
It, groaning thing,
Turned black and sank.
Then from the far caverns
Of dead sins
Came monsters, livid with desire.
They fought,
Wrangled over the world,
A morsel.
But of all sadness this was sad —
A woman's arms tried to shield
The head of a sleeping man
From the jaws of the final beast.

LXVIII

A spirit sped
Through spaces of night;
And as he sped, he called,
"God! God!"
He went through valleys
Of black death-slime,
Ever calling,
"God! God!"
Their echoes
From crevice and cavern
Mocked him:
"God! God! God!"
Fleetly into the plains of space

He went, ever calling,
"God! God!"
Eventually, then, he screamed,
Mad in denial,
"Ah, there is no God!"

A swift hand,
A sword from the sky,
Smote him,
And he was dead.

WAR IS KIND.

DO NOT WEEP, MAIDEN, FOR WAR IS KIND.
BECAUSE YOUR LOVER THREW WILD HANDS
   TOWARD THE SKY
AND THE AFFRIGHTED STEED RAN ON ALONE,
DO NOT WEEP.
WAR IS KIND.

HOARSE, BOOMING DRUMS OF THE REGIMENT,
LITTLE SOULS WHO THIRST FOR FIGHT,
THESE MEN WERE BORN TO DRILL AND DIE.
THE UNEXPLAINED GLORY FLIES ABOVE THEM,
GREAT IS THE BATTLE-GOD, GREAT, AND HIS
   KINGDOM —
A FIELD WHERE A THOUSAND CORPSES LIE.

DO NOT WEEP, BABE, FOR WAR IS KIND.
BECAUSE YOUR FATHER TUMBLED IN THE
   YELLOW TRENCHES,
RAGED AT HIS BREAST, GULPED AND DIED,
DO NOT WEEP.
WAR IS KIND.

SWIFT BLAZING FLAG OF THE REGIMENT,
EAGLE WITH CREST OF RED AND GOLD,
THESE MEN WERE BORN TO DRILL AND DIE.
POINT FOR THEM THE VIRTUE OF SLAUGHTER,
MAKE PLAIN TO THEM THE EXCELLENCE OF
   KILLING
AND A FIELD WHERE A THOUSAND CORPSES LIE.

MOTHER WHOSE HEART HUNG HUMBLE AS A
    BUTTON
ON THE BRIGHT SPLENDID SHROUD OF YOUR SON,
DO NOT WEEP.
WAR IS KIND.

CPSIA information can be obtained at www.ICGtesting.com
Printed in the USA
BVOW071132190812

298250BV00001B/52/P